Copyright © 2021 Tekkan
Artwork Copyright © 2021

All rights reserved.
First Printing, 2021
ISBN 978-1-7363537-0-7

To contact Tekkan please email:
buddhaboy1289@gmail.com

Table of Contents

Dino Derby . . . . Page 22

Clouds . . . . Page 58

Tyrannosaurs in Requiem . . . . Page 88

This book is for Fran, who gives me many good ideas for poems.

How to Read My Poems

I have married the sonnet to the tanka. I tell a story in the sonnet — using three quatrains separated by line spaces, and a final couplet. The story builds to a conclusion in the couplet. The tanka is a commentary, or a counterpoint, to the sonnet — the combined poems have two endings.

I don't usually rhyme my sonnets, because I want freer expression. I want to be direct in my meaning — I want people to clearly understand my meaning. The metaphors are inspired by Shakespeare, and the (aimed-for) precision is in imitation of Japanese style. Using the sonnet with the tanka, I mix the sensibility of the Occident and the Orient — which I have done by living in England, Japan, and America.

I don't punctuate much in my poetry. I want the words themselves to do the work. There is inherent logic between words, and the forms provide structure. By not using punctuation I hope to direct readers to carefully attend to each word — to appreciate the graininess of words.

Reading my poems silently, say, on a bus, a train, or an airplane, and reading them aloud, may be different experiences. The way I've written, there's not always a pause intended at the end of the line.

Hint: *My poems are to be recited not as lines but as phrases, and a phrase often overflows the break at the end of a line. I pause and take a breath where it seems natural for me to pause. Another person may pause differently than I do.*

Each single poem is a piece of a mosaic, and it is my hope that the collection of poems forms an accurate portrait of consciousness.

My daughter, Jocelyn MacDonald, is a wonderful artist. Her artwork graces this book.

I am Barry MacDonald. I received the *dharma* name *Tekkan*, which means "Iron Man," a settled practitioner of great determination.

— *Tekkan*

Everyday Mind XVIII

A chill arises with
fresh fallen snow
felt in the folds
of my jeans making me
alert.

It's remarkable how much depends on
The artificial demarcation of
New Year's Day as we do regiment our
Accounting of taxable income with

The closing of December 31st
And the starting of January 1st
And everyone wants to have a party
Celebrating another New Year on

The journey to senility because
What could we do otherwise than to choose
Frivolity over melancholy
As we need to have a ceremony

For passing time because we are human
And are compulsive at measuring things.

Getting plastered drunk
on New Year's Eve
and sobering up on
New Year's Day is
what we do.

I assert my liberation to mark
The passage of seasons according to
My predilections and on the verge of
Another blizzard of necessity

I raise my perspective from the prospect
Of the dull continuing routine of
Shovel snow blower and city snowplow
To the horizon of distant April

When Arctic temperatures are finished
And gritty grime-encrusted heaps of snow
Are melted when the sparkle of the sun
Begins to grow the grass and bud the trees

And when the glowing cups of the tulips
Are blooming and radiating sunlight.

Tulips are
resurrected
in April splashing
a barren landscape
with brilliance.

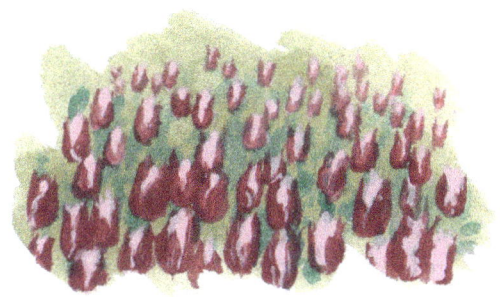

Kitcat was flicking his tail under the
Closed bathroom door while I was shaving and
When I seized it he began swiping his
Paw beneath the door as I was busy

With the razor attending to my face
Reinforcing an idea of who
I am by gazing in the mirror and
Hypnotizing myself with my image

When I realized that Kitcat doesn't
Have a conception of what he looks like
And he turns his head when I show him his
Body in the mirror and he is free of

Obsessional and sophisticated
Self-regard and he is mischievous.

He is frolicsome
while I can't imagine
getting by without
peering in mirrors.

I'm used to watching the sun cresting the
Horizon from my desk through the window
And in summer I can shut my eyes and
Determine the exact location of

The sun by sensing its pulsating heat
While during winter the sky is often
Overcome with a layer of white clouds
Tinged with gray and usually the sun

Is hidden but yesterday afternoon
While driving amid the freshly fallen
Snow I saw within an overcast sky
A white blazing disk of sunlight shorn of

Summer prominence but emanating
Enough light to clarify everything.

A gleaming
disk in the sky
has enough blaze
to keep the world
alive.

I listen to recordings of Alan
Watts who was a beatnik guru as I'm
Driving to the post office or Aldi's
Grocery store and though Alan has died

Decades ago he is a companion
Entertaining and enlightening me
With the lore and *dharma* of the ancient
Indians Chinese and Japanese with

Eloquence witty and humorous in
A cultured British accent and I have
Greedily attended scrutinizing
Every word and phrasing while intending

To saturate my being with him and
I've also heard him absentmindedly.

All the familiar
streets and highways
in all the seasons
are mixed up
with Alan's words.

Alan doesn't the minimize the horrors
And complexities of life but he turns
The context around revealing that each
Of us is an imperishable node

Of a cosmos observing itself and
Partaking in every sight sound and
Taste and when I experience the range
Of emotions confounded discouraged

Satisfied or absentminded I am
A universe at a point of ceaseless
Becoming evolving and emerging
With fresh circumstances and if only

I could drop my victimized perspective
I would be liberated from the past.

I don't completely
understand Alan
but he inspires
irrepressible
intuitive joy.

At our meeting in Pioneer Park when
The air is 6 degrees Fahrenheit one
Of us says that she is happy to be
Up before dawn with each of us because

It's important on New Year's Day to start
The first morning of another year off
On the right footing as we could have been
Passed out in bed and sleeping off a drunk

But we are clear-headed and bright-eyed and
Exuberant around a cheery fire
In a portable container recounting
All our blessings energizing ourselves as

We are observing the darkness dissipate
On a cloudless day with fresh fallen snow.

The branches and twigs
of the broad and tall
bur oak in Pioneer Park
appear to be scratching
the open sky.

When opening my refrigerator
Door and retrieving a container I
Find a ripe plenitude of overlarge
Blueberries inside of a plastic box

That I did buy a couple days ago
Without noticing the quality of
The produce within a busy day while
I was attending to many details

Plopping bananas and oranges and
Milk within my cart and too harried to
Appreciate the bounty awaiting
My attention until this morning when

I exuberate gratefully over
Finding such elephantine blueberries.

Usually blueberries
coming all the way
from Chile in winter
are hard and
pea-sized.

I am also grateful this morning for
Running into my gym buddy Greg at
Walmart where he passed on the word that the
Gym has reopened but because of the

Ongoing pandemic and a mandate
From government everyone throughout the
Building at all times must be wearing a
Mask during even the most heart-pumping

And breathtaking vigorous exercise
Which would be such a drag and a drain but
Not for me because a month ago I
Spotted an inexpensive and sturdy

Stationary bike inside a box that
I fortuitously bought at Walmart.

I can get happily
sweaty every day
without wearing
a mask in my
living room.

I am grateful that the temperature
Is in the low 20s and I hope that
The air continues to be so because
The snowfalls are fluffy and the snow is

Easy to move when the snow blowers are
Prepared and are a snap to start in the
Colder weather but the fresh fallen snow
Is spoiled by urinating dogs grimed by

Salt-spewing snowplows and the everyday
Traffic and trodden on by the squirrels
And worst of all the integrity of
My cleared driveway is cluttered by the gunk

Of the collected snow in my wheel wells
When the disgusting glop falls from my car.

After so many winters
all the details of the
season are
indelible.

Henry David Thoreau remarked on the
Quiet desperation that people live
Within and I interpret his words
To mean a sense of isolation and

A disposition to keep emotions
And disharmony shut within a stream
Of private thought compounding over time
Till a separation between self and

Other seems unbridgeable perhaps not
Encompassing every aspect of life
And not hindering casual give and
take but so regarding the desperate

Desire for communication and a
Mutual understanding and for love.

I testify to a
numbness
concealing
grief and sadness
with anger.

Alan says a poet can talk about
Anything and he describes the Hindu
Myth of presenting existence on the
Human level as a game of hide and

Seek wherein the divine says to people
Get lost and so with disharmony and
Dissatisfaction we do get lost with
An underlying intuition that

There is a happy union to be found
Creating a dynamic below the
Level of conscious awareness seeking
For wholeness which is the divine in us

Camouflaged within a vulnerable
Ego questing for a liberation.

Is my skin a
barrier or a bridge
between me and the
world as everything seems
to get inside of me?

Imagine the pages of a book to
Assume the aspect of the moments of
A life in which there are continuous
Zaps of insight as they are the sparks of

The divine maybe not the encompassed
Union of liberation but of fire-
Flies of understanding and of bite-sized
Portions of recognition presenting

How joyful overlarge blueberries are
How zestful predawn conversation is
And how year after year winter blizzards
Make a pattern burdensome but also

Beautiful when described as cycle of
Dormancy and then of resurrection.

I assume
everyday
something
is worth
communicating.

Each poem of mine contains only a
Single period after I've reached a
Tentative just-for-today conclusion
Before which is a compendium of

Turning phrases creating a single
Run-on sentence and there's no reason or
Rhyme for writing sonnets the way I do
Except that it's fun to express in a

Package of verbiage something worthy of
Expression perhaps balancing meaning
Maybe in a daring experiment
To test whether I can spur a reader's

Curiosity to the end before
The words collapse into jabberwocky.

After a while
arbitrary
pattern
assumes
a compulsion.

There are the winter days of blue skies and
Sparkling snow when the sun lights millions of
Bitty crystals and the snow is fresh and
Yet untouched and the trees are posturing

Revealed in their millions of gesturing
Crooks and angles unsymmetrical and
Dominating the landscape and frosted
With a thinnest tinge of snow and branches

And twigs are crisscrossing the drifting of
Snow with wild shadows interspersing a
Blanketing of the snow with patterns of
Purest light and gray wherein the more I

Look the more I see near and far pinpoint
Brilliant jewels refracting rainbow sunlight.

Drab overcast days
metamorphize with
open skies
fresh fallen snow
crisp air.

I've been alerted over the phone by
My girlfriend who has expert medical
Knowledge that it's not the dust itself or
Even the dust mites that everyone is

Allergic to but it is the feces
Produced by the dust mites that causes the
Calamity and I didn't mention
The congestion within my lungs or the

Stuffiness in my nose but she could tell
And I wasn't even aware of my
Condition until she told me and the
Casual tone with which she spoke as she

Revealed the mite-sized menaces lurking
In my rooms was shockingly effective.

I simply had to
bring out paper towels
glass cleaner
a broom and a
vacuum cleaner.

Stretching upon my bed
I try to drain my head
I blow my nose
And close my eyes
But can't stop sneezing instead.

Perhaps the mix of sensations involved
In a sneeze surpasses description and
One or even a series of sneezes
While I am sitting in a Zen posture

Calm and alert and apart from others
Where sneezing is without consequence is
Not so awful but during a viral
Pandemic when liquid begins sloshing

Within my nasal cavity with an
Ominous tickle in the nose that brings
A sudden light-headed anxiety
In the company of people — then I

Know with a dreadful certainty that a
Sneeze is coming and it can't be stopped.

Do I take the mask off
or leave it on?

We have something that the ancient Chinese
Poets didn't when they looked at the moon
And made it a symbol of mystery
And untouchable beauty as we have

The Apollo rockets and the Lunar
Rover and we know that moon dust smells like
Burnt charcoal similar to ashes from
A fire and our astronauts have trodden

On the orb without a sky and planted
A flag within the abominable
And the eternal silence of the moon
And we have seen that the scarring on the

Surface is a testimony for a
Propensity of cosmic violence.

The moon remains
a beautiful symbol
of untouchable
emptiness which
the poets understood.

I used to think that to be up on the
News in America I had to read
The daily articles commentating
On current events but now I see that

The reports are a repetition of
Violence scandal and tragedy and
That most of the information gleaned is
Gossipy distorted and deceitful

And that to gain an understanding of
What's really happening I have to trust
A few commentators who have proven
To be trustworthy over many years

Because nobody is capable of
Telling only facts minus opinions.

The doings of
mass numbers of
people are almost
incomprehensible.

Dino Derby

This creature's body stretched 40 feet from
Snout to tail which is about the length of
A school bus — standing 12 feet and weighing
8 tons and its gargantuan jaws could

Crush a car and a stiff skull allowed it
To channel all its Herculean force
Into the muscles of a bite with 6
Tons of pressure with 60 serrated

Teeth 8 inches long to pierce and grip flesh
Throwing an animal into the air
And swallowing it whole and it plodded
Forward headfirst on two mighty legs but

It possessed two puny arms that may have
Been evolutionary leftovers.

A large portion of
of the brain of
Tyrannosaurus Rex
was devoted to smell
similar to house cats.

This dinosaur had an enormous skull
With a backward pointing frill extending
In length up to 7 feet which had a
Thin flap of skin that stretched over solid

Bone and perhaps the whole formation of
The skull served as a device to display
Sexual dominance as the frill would
Flush pink with many blood vessels in its

Skin and it was an herbivore about
The size of a cow with 2 pointy horns
And a horn on its nose and a parrot-
Like beak which could clip vegetation and

It could chew with a few hundred shearing
Teeth within replaceable rows of teeth.

In marshes and forests of
western North America
Triceratops may
have been food
for T-Rex.

The Sinclair Oil Corporation uses
This dinosaur as its logo and the
Post Office put its image on stamps and
It must have had a mighty heart and high

Blood pressure to pump blood all the way up
Its long neck and it took 10 years to reach
Adult size — stretching 72 feet
Long — standing 15 feet high at the hips —

Weighing 17 tons — living as long
As 100 years — laying 12-inch eggs —
And breathing through nostrils on the top of
Its head and it was an herbivore that

Ate lots of vegetation and swallowed
Stones to help digestion in its stomach.

Scientists argue over
its name but currently
this thunder lizard
is called the
Brontosaurus.

Paleontologists call its spiked tail
A "thagomizer" in special honor
Of a Far Side cartoon and because of
The row of upstanding plates along its

Back — and because moviemakers added a
Tyrannosaur bite — it incarnated
Cinematic magic as "Godzilla"
And it stretched 29 feet long and weighed

5 to 7 tons and stood 9 feet tall
And lived 75 to 100 years
And it was an herbivore with a brain
Mass comparable with a walnut quite

Equivalent in size to Kitcat's brain
And Kitcat regularly outsmarts me.

Stegosaurus lives
in the imagination
of movie makers
cartoonists and
paleontologists.

This creature was a winged lizard and its
Young were dubbed flaplings by our whimsical
Paleontologists and it was a
Carnivore eating small animals and

Fish with an elongated beak fringed with
90 razor-sharp teeth believed to be
Active during the day — living 10 to
25 years — weighing 2 to 10 pounds —

And about 3½ feet in length —
With a wingspan of 3½ feet —
Discovered in Bavaria almost
250 years ago — and it

Waddled about on the earth on back legs
And with fingers on pointed leather wings.

Pterodactyl is
pronounced with a
silent "P" and means
winged finger.

This was an armored dinosaur and was
Considered a "fused lizard" because of
The bony plates on its back which are dubbed
Scutes and osteoderms and it ambled

About on four legs around 6 miles an
Hour — eating foliage — living 70
To 80 years — weighing 2 to 8 tons —
Stretching 20 to 26 feet long —

And it is thought to have had a good sense
Of smell and on the end of its tail there
Was a walloping and a whacking club
Which it could swing forcefully enough to

Shatter the bones of the toothier brutes
Which is why it is called a living tank.

The carnivores
would have had to flip
Ankylosaurus
over to get at its
underbelly.

These dinosaurs were pack hunters and lost
Out in our time because their name is hard
To pronounce and they could only trot at
6 miles an hour but the Hollywood

Moviemakers seized upon the razor-
Sharp second toe large curving talon that
Could inflict huge gashing wounds and their bite
Was like an alligator's chomping with

60 sharp teeth and they were 11
Feet long and weighed 220 pounds
And stood about 3 feet at the hip and
Maybe they had feathers but they were not

So smart as to be able to turn door
Knobs as they are portrayed in the movies.

Deinonychus
is pronounced
dyn-NON-ik-us —
nowhere near as cool as
Velociraptor.

Velociraptors were about the size
Of small turkeys as long as 6.8
Feet from snout to tail — weighing 33
To 43 pounds — standing at about

1½ feet tall — and they could sprint
40 miles an hour and they could jump
As they hunted but they didn't hunt in
Packs as portrayed in movies and their snouts

Were long and narrow with serrated teeth
And they ran on two toes on each of two
Legs retracting a sickle talon on
Each foot and they had two arms and hands with

Three curving claws on each hand and they ate
Small amphibians reptiles and insects.

Velociraptors had
Feathers — and raptor
means robber and
Velociraptor means
swift thief.

This animal was one of the largest
To roam the earth being 69 to
75 feet long — 15 feet high at
The hips — weighing 18 to 25

Tons and scientists debate about the
Flexibility of its 40-foot
Neck arguing whether it could lift its
Neck to eat the foliage at the top of

The tree canopy but they are certain
That it could swing and snap its 50-foot
Tail like a bullwhip terrorizing its
Foes producing a sonic crack like a

Cannon blast but now the snapping sound is
Gone and we can only imagine it.

Western North America
150 million
years ago was the scene
of Apatosaurus'
whipping crack.

In one of the "Jurassic Park" movies
A Spinosaurus has a slashing and
Toothy engagement with a T-Rex and
Snaps the T-Rex's neck and though it is

True the Spinosaurus is larger and
Has a cool-looking sail upon its back
Paleontologists observe that its
Jaws were not as mighty and its teeth were

Much smaller than T-Rex's teeth and yet
Spinosaurus did have a cruel set of
Claws 6 to 8 inches long capable
Of inflicting deep gashes but most of

The experts conclude Spinosaurus was
No match for T-Rex's terrible jaws.

The two creatures
lived at different
times and places —
Spino in North Africa
T-Rex in North America.

Since we have been unearthing their remains
We have given so much energetic
Imagination to recreating
Life as the dinosaurs must have lived it

Millions of years ago expending our
Fancy and speculation but I can't
Imagine the dinosaurs brainstorming
About us and figuring out what kind

Of animals we would be — so what kind
Of bizarre and otherworldly beings
Will be digging up our bones and fussing
Over us and puzzling about the fine

Details of our capabilities and
Will they discover our stupidity?

We live in a cosmos
of trillions of
galaxies beyond
anyone's
imagination.

What would it be like to be afraid that
The doctors don't care about you and that
The vaccine for the pandemic virus
Isn't intended to save but to kill

You because you are black and you aren't on
The priority list and also to
Be sure that the police are dangerous
And that the justice system is crooked

And to be surrounded by people who
Are thinking the same way reinforcing
A terrified isolated state of
Mind only somewhat relieved by reading

The Holy Bible that speaks about what
Is happening around you on this day?

The world seems
quite different
from various points
and I can't say
she is wrong.

After we started by reading aloud
From a book about letting go of the
Troubles of yesterday and tomorrow
And of fighting the battles of just one

Day — today — because anyone can face
The difficulties of just one day it
Is healthy to keep my mouth shut and
To listen as everyone takes a turn

In the circle speaking about what is
Going on today because I see how
Differently each of us is thinking
And how I create burdens for myself

Because I tend to believe what I think
And it is good to practice listening.

My thoughts may
become an endless
labyrinth but by
listening I find
today.

The pandemic is keeping people from
Mixing in light-hearted ways and a fear
Of infection is putting the entire
Country on edge as each of us knows of

Someone who caught the virus and there
Are deaths but life is continuing with
The stipulation that we keep 6 feet
Between each other in businesses and

In stores while wearing masks for whatever
Debatable good they do but most of
My sustaining communication is
Done face to face among a handful of

People and the words that we exchange are
Precious moments of camaraderie.

Messages coming over
computer screens
televisions
and videos
foster paranoia.

My moments of camaraderie give
Me the grace to see beyond my fears and
Frustrations to the cosmic mysteries
Wherein our political contretemps

And our pandemic virus are only
Storms fitting entirely within the
The drama and disorientation
Of a human world and maybe all the

Fuss is like a chaotic dream forcing
My adaptation and evolution —
And the balancing of my consciousness
Is a taste of cosmic play so that I

Experience the wild and outrageous
Emotions on the way to somewhere else.

Maybe I was an
Apatosaurus swinging
a mighty bullwhip tail
150 million
years ago.

This moment contains all the galaxies
And all the motions of the galaxies
And all of their suns and their planets too —
Orbits within orbits within orbits —

This is the moment of becoming when
Something new and fresh is arising
And you need not believe that what comes is
Bound by the past but you may dare to seek

A liberation perhaps not apart
From pain and disorientation or
Even terror but through difficulty
And then maybe a new freedom will come

As easily as an apple falling
From a tree — metamorphosis arrives.

Be poised
open
patient
calm
ready.

Kitcat's whiskers are unbelievable
Having supersensitive tips able
To pick up vibrations within the dark
Letting him know which objects to avoid

Whether he can fit inside of a box
Or inside of the cupboard above my
Refrigerator — and summer breezes
Coming through the screened windows of my home

Send him messages of animals in
The neighborhood and of when a rainstorm
Is approaching — and the follicles are
Deeply embedded in his skin with nerve

Endings electrically signaling his
Awareness with a touching kind of radar.

Did a Tyrannosaur
have whiskers?

These pages are like the days of a life
Bound together with a memory of
Dubious reliability with
Each page containing the brilliance of a

Summer day arising from the paper
Consisting of the texture of a tree
That in its day was tasting the sunlight
And drinking rainwater and minerals

With its roots and whatever words can do
Upon the substance of a page to bring
To life a moment of insight and joy
The expression is worthy of a life-

Time's effort in preparation for just
A moment of carefree exploration.

Beyond the
intensity and
infinity of
this moment
there is mystery.

Love and care are essential for making
A piano and a craftsman will use
Various woods like birch mahogany
Oak ebony spruce and maple and it

Takes an expert eye to choose the straight-grained
Woods without knots and patience to air dry
The wood over six months to two years and
Virtuosity of knowledge and skill

In fitting the best wood for a precise
Function as the soundboard is made of spruce
Because spruce is quite elastic and the
Maker knows in which season to harvest

The wood when it contains the least amount
Of sap and with about 10 years of growth.

Love in transition —
the studio piano
in my living room
from her grandfather
to my daughter is
waiting for space.

The playing of a taut string via the
Bridge and nut passes to the body of
The instrument where the panels of
The violin reverberate thusly

Emitting lovely waves of sound and the
Quality of music is affected
By the rigidity of connection
Between the bridge and the panels and the

Types of wood are crucial with spruce for the
Top and willow for the internal blocks
And linings and maple for the back and
Ribs and neck and the traditional "s"-

Shaped holes on the front of the body of
The violin make a resonation.

The musician
refines herself
with creative
discipline to
play joyfully.

The wet heavy snow overnight was not
As much as forecasted but was enough for
Me to rearrange a hectic schedule
To focus on the most necessary

Chores and both of my snow blowers on both
Of the driveways were able to move the
Snow as it was melting in the machines
Becoming water demonstrating that

What doesn't work on a given day may
Surprisingly produce miracles on a
Another day and I am left without
An explanation especially when

I'm often crabby when much too busy
But today I was cheerfully engaged.

Today I am grateful
to be able to use
my arms and legs
and snow blowers
to good purpose.

The voice of a harp arises from the
Plucking of the differently sized strings
Making the vibrations of higher and
Lower frequency and the playing of

The strings pushes energy onto the
Curving soundboard making vibrations of
Ascending and descending quality
And when vibrations ascend air rushes

Into the shape of the harp and when the
Vibrations descend air pushes out of
Its shape and out of the air holes along
The straight back of the instrument and the

Rippling pressures entering eardrums
With tasteful frequency make the music.

The harp is depicted
in images inside of
Egyptian and
Mesopotamian
tombs and produces
tears laughter and sleep.

The accumulation of overcast
Days with the blanketing of snow on the
Ground with the opacity of the sky
And the drab gray/brown of the leafless trees

Imposes a weariness over the
Season wherein the details of the days
Merge together in memory after
A somewhat happy day of moving snow

Off of driveways I know that yesterday
Will dissolve as surely as one falling
Of snow will blend with the snow on the ground
Without a seam as the streets become a

Patchwork of cleared asphalt and ice and the
Chickadees and the crows are spicing days.

After 24 years of
moving snow the
corners of my
iron shovel are
rusted and curled.

When I'm meditating he sleeps on the
Couch in the living room with me and he
Will sometimes while I'm meditating sprawl
And stretch out on the rug in front of me

Just to distract my attention and on
Saturday and on Sunday the only
Days when I don't set the alarm at 5
A.m. he will yowl and cavort on the

Bed much earlier than I intend to
Get up and if I don't get out of bed
Then he will jump on the chest of drawers and
Lick and nibble on the peacock feathers

That I keep in a marble urn because
He knows exactly how to annoy me.

Brushing Kitcat
after I leave bed is the
pinnacle of the
day when he wrestles
yowls and bites.

I was enlightened while digging up the
Information necessary to write
Poetry about dinosaurs when I read
That both cats and Tyrannosaurus Rex

Have an ample percentage of their brains
Devoted to a sense of smell and with
A new awareness I've been watching how
Kitcat will sniff just about everything

Over again including my hands and
Maybe my hands do smell differently
At various times which naturally
Leads me to imagine a curious

And rather insistent Tyrannosaur
Sniffing my hands which isn't very nice.

My living room
is much too small
to contain a T-Rex.

There is the belief that whatever we
Obsess over we draw into our lives
And I think I am safe concerning an
Obsequious Tyrannosaurus Rex

And I also believe haphazardly
Without quite intending it I've gotten
Better at attracting beneficial
Instead of detrimental involvements

Into my experience because I
Spend so much of my time cogitating
Mostly curious and optimistic
Poetry as I am hunting for those

Special moments happening everyday
That are worthy of a celebration.

The little red squirrel
that I watch run along
the top of the white fence
down the hill *came* to the hedge
just outside of my window.

Even during the somnolent season
When the ground is blanketed with the snow
And the sky is so often overcast
Outside my window where I am typing

On my keyboard and composing my thoughts
The days are peppered with inspiration
As the hedge trimmed below the windowsill
Is little more than a foot from me and

Within these couple of hours today
The little red squirrel and a female
Cardinal and three differently marked
Chickadees came to peek at me moving

As they do in jerky hopping motions
And they linger only a few seconds.

It's easy to spot
simple marvels
within
eyesight.

What would it be like to be a writer
For the Hollywood entertainment crowd
Dreaming up the scenarios and the
Dialogue for daily situation

Comedies or the soap operas or
The late-night talk shows as it would become
A daunting challenge to come up with fresh
Material garnered from everyday

Events of a quality to enthrall
The type of audience patronizing
Such shows as a writer would be impelled
To shoehorn his consciousness inside of

The ridiculous and the exploitive
The snarky corrosive and prurient?

Is making people laugh
serious
exhausting
dispiriting
drudgery?

I would like to believe myself to be
Above the prurient and corrosive
Influences of the entertainment
Industry but I am as attracted

To sarcasm as anyone is and
I admit that watching T.V. is like
Ingesting too much sugar inspiring
A temporary thrill but leading to

A depressing eventuality
So I usually confine myself
To murder investigations starting
With a gruesome mystery proceeding

With a determined pursuit of the clues
And concluding with righteous judgment.

My head is cluttered
with stories inside
stories inside
stories.

We are connected to our culture with
The Internet and are saturated
With narratives of acceptable and
Disfavored opinions and people have

Been led to distrust the "conspiracy
Theories" but each of us inherits a
Core set of beliefs honestly and we
Add to our understanding as best we

Can but these days the invective and the
Raw hatred expressed by the combatting
Parties is at an extreme and it seems
Impossible to escape bitterness

Disorientation and suspicion
As it's difficult to know whom to trust.

It's easier among
my friends who have
various opinions
not to talk about
certain topics.

I am connected to the Internet
Gathering information and doing
Business and driving about every day
With a smartphone inside of my pocket

And Google Facebook and Amazon are
Collecting information and tracking
My whereabouts and are following my
Use of the Internet as one of three

Hundred million Americans and
I do assume that with such a massive
Number of people that I have privacy
And protective anonymity with

Nothing to fear no reason for worry
As who would care about how I'm living?

Our sophisticated
information
society is
increasingly
interconnected.

If I am not carefully watching the
Power of my thinking I will become
A mighty iron freight engine pulling
A weighty train of cars and each car will

Encapsulate a memory of a
Vanished opportunity or of an
Argument involving bitter words or
A rehearsal of justifications

And my mighty engine will run along
The iron rails of negativity
Oblivious to the liberation
That comes with simple relaxation as

For some reason it is easy to be
Angry but so difficult to relax.

When I am lost
in a memory I'm
not using my
eyes to see or
my ears to hear.

There are always details to attend to
And chores of necessity to finish
And snares of difficulty and if I
Worry I can be like Alice falling

Down an endless rabbit hole and dreading
A hard landing but this morning snow is
Curving to the ground in tiny grains and
The flakes are meandering and lazy

And there isn't any wind and the air
Is much colder today as it should be
In January which means that the snow
Will be light and easy to move and now

I am watching the snow mix with the sky
And the meandering snow is the sky.

The snow/sky
or sky/snow
is glowing
white with
sunlight.

I have to take off the elephantine
Mittens to press the tiny button of
The car keys to open the door of the
Car and then I buckle the seatbelt with

My hands and insert the key into the
Ignition and start the car and I put
On the mittens again because of
The cold but soon I get to the office

And take off the mittens to press on the
Button of the garage door opener
And I exit the car opening doors
With one hand holding stapled papers and

The two thermoses of coffee and the
Two mittens with the other handy hand.

I press the thermoses
and stapled papers
to my body under
the crook of a
bent elbow.

My kids are grown and are making their way
In the world and they have my affection —
My ex-wife and I are living apart
After having raised our kids together

And she and I are better off apart —
And the weight of the care of having a
Family earning a precarious
Income making repairs as best I could

Schooling the kids celebrating birthdays
Taking vacations lying awake in
Bed with worry about their struggles and
Their health — all these apprehensions have passed —

My solitary putzing about the
House is assuming a Zen quietude.

I talk with friends
see birds
apple blossoms
autumn leaves
shadows on snow.

Driving along the street to the office
Which I do absentmindedly daily
I am seeing this morning the line of
Oaks and cottonwoods bordering the street

As the sun is cresting the horizon
To the right and I don't see rays of
Light in the air but I do see the bare
Trees bathed in a glow of orange sunlight

And I am the only one present as
The street is empty of traffic and hushed
And for some reason I am impacted
By the light with joyful solemnity

As if all my burdens were lifted for
A moment by a touch of loveliness.

Glimpsing beauty
amid a drab
landscape — joy
takes me.

Clouds

Stratus — low layering horizontal
Cirrus — wispy curling locks of hair
Stratocumulus — large dark rounded and low
Cumulonimbus — towering vertical thunderheads
Cumulus — cottonlike
Altostratus — gray to bluish-green layers
Nimbostratus — continuous rain snow sleet
Altocumulus — globs masses patches
Cirrocumulus — high patches and rows
Cirrostratus — high thin diffuse

We name the
continuous drama
of earth sun
oceans rivers
atmosphere.

The saying goes that the Great Way isn't
Difficult for those without preferences
As it is a disease of the mind to
Cherish opinions arguing against

Offensive ideas with opposing
Ideas endlessly and even the
Burning intensity of love propels
Its opposite hate which corrodes the heart

Dispirits equanimity and I
Understand the wording of the "Heart/Mind"
Sutra asserting that once the mind is
Emptied everything else vanishes but

I can't see how meditation empties
The mind or if I want to be empty.

I enjoy
coffee
with cream.

It is easy to believe that I am
Somebody going somewhere doing my
Best to make someone of myself and with
Extra effort I can accomplish a

Goal and afterward I will relax and
Be proud of myself as I can vaguely
Remember a beginning and I am
Certain there's an ending and now I seem

To be somewhere in the middle but for
Some reason the poetry breaks
The rules as there isn't a narrative
Binding poems together but rather

Every poem is curiosity
Tasting and savoring differing vibes.

Maybe I am
a conscious
ripple within
ripples within
ripples.

The crows aren't bothered by the arctic cold
As they don't feel the need to move about
As they are busy perching in the oak
As light is rising from the horizon

Behind them and they get my attention
By vibrating air with their voices and
I notice the rippling resonance in
The air and I see them perching on what

Seem to me the thinnest of the twigs of
The bur oak and I realize that the
Crows know better than I how much weight a
Twig will bear and suddenly one of the

Crows leaves the oak and flies to a maple
Perhaps to sound his voice from over there.

The two crows
in the park
at sunrise
are a joy
this morning.

It's been pointed out to me that I am
Not as affectionate as I could be
As I appear emotionally distant and
Reserved in person and I know it's true

And I feel an awkward self-consciousness
About touching and embracing others
And even though I'm able to smile in
Carefree conversation it's difficult

To relax and put on a natural
Expression for a photograph so I
Sport at best a grin or look impassive
Because somehow I've become defensive

And I'm wearing a suit of armor as
A tool against vulnerability.

Unlearning
unconscious
unintentional
habits is
tricky.

The words are skipping across the paper
In a horizontal fashion from the
Left and to the right and the words are a
Trick manipulating you my reader

To follow the flow of the words to form
The syllables silently perhaps and
To register ideas as you are
Shifting your eyes from left to right reaching

The end of a line and dropping to the
Line below following a train of thought
Anticipating by now where is this
Package of verbiage leading and what

Is its purpose and what does it really mean
And I will say it's just a dance of words . . .

. . . as the seconds
and the minutes and
the hours are just a
dance of days.

An overcast winter sky resembles
The whiteness of a page with an added
Tinge of gray and the bareness of the trees
Is similar to letters on a page

Because the dark branches and black letters
Appear upon a white background and the
Contrast is rather stark but the letters
Are symmetrical and regimented

And the words are logical and carry
Meaning — at least the meaning is implied —
Whereas the forms of the trees under a
Winter sky have no symmetry at all

And maybe their twisting and crooked forms
Epitomize wild creativity.

The nonsymmetrical
wild creativity
evolved into logic
but what does that
mean?

According to scientists maybe the
Most telling act of creativity
Within the more than four billion years of
The spinning Earth was accomplished by a

Prokaryote which is a single-celled
Organism possessing a membrane
But not a nucleus which was the first
Living organism that somehow learned

To use its body to catch photons from
The sun creating photosynthesis
Starting the ball rolling without a brain
Or eyes or hands or blueprints and without

Any foresight or consciousness and thus
All of our complexities have blossomed.

All the questions
scientists can
dream of
originated from
a senseless blob.

So did the chickadee pecking about
In the hedge outside of my window come
Into the world from somewhere else or did
The chickadee come out of the world

And did I projecting as I do a
Frolicsome curiosity and a
Burdensome load of anxiety come
Into the world from somewhere else or did

I come out of the world as a consequence
Of a cosmic eruption emerging
From incomprehensible nothingness
Proceeding with orbits within orbits

Ripples within ripples within ripples
And destined to return to nothingness?

Is nothingness itself
somewhere else
or is it here?

After a powder snow the white of snow
And the white sky and the white of the page
Overwhelm the neighborhood coating the
Needles of the pines and the branches of

The trees and concealing the grime and grit
Filling bootprints and squirrel tracks and I
Yank the cord start the blower raise its front
Pull back and turn directing it squeezing

Its handles engaging its rotor blades
And I am methodically plowing
The snow in straight lines just like the words of
This poem as the words are progressing

From the left to the right I am pacing
Happily clearing the driveway of snow.

Snow covers everything
I plow the snow
in straight lines
and type words
in straight lines.

A fresh falling of snow erases the
Accumulating mess that snow becomes
Over winter days and the crud that drops
From the wheel wells of cars is hidden and

The pitting and misshaping that thawing
And freezing does to snow on the ground is
Covered and when the sky clears again then
Suddenly the trees are casting patterns

Of wild shadows across the pristine snow
And sunlight descending from an open
Sky is sparking embedded crystals of snow
Making pinpoint gleams of green blue and red

And then the snow is appearing to be
An enchanting mesmerizing blanket.

But even inside a
house I have to wear
thick winter socks
to warm
my toes.

"Woo" is a wonderful word for the art
Of persuasion in love when a lover
Is possessed by a passion enraptured
Dazzled besotted with a beloved

And wooing is a multiplication
Of adoration during the day and
Of enticing exciting entwining
Dreams in the night and to woo is be

Captured by "foo" and when one is moved to
Wooing it's all based upon a fooing
Without a smidgeon of moderation
And when I am wooing it is because

I can't escape from the fooing and all
Of my awareness is consumed with foo.

I don't believe
it's possible to
woo unless one
is saturated with
foo.

Someone should not spend too much of his time
Doing business under the influence
Of foo because foo is nonsensical
And foo is befuddlement and when one

Is apart from his rationality
One is liable to foozle over
A crazy choice of words and to foozle
In using his money and one might say

That fooing and wooing lead directly
To foozlement because when one is in
Love sobriety is an afterthought
And it's not unheard of for someone to

Be foozling haphazardly and I
Can attest to my own share of foozle.

Can you imagine
a woozy
foozy
doctor
judge
scientist
politician?

I am not a propitious judge of
The worthiness of my conversation
Of the clarity of my editing
Or of the value of my poetry

Because on occasion I assume that
My facility of expression is
Jubilant and the words are of themselves
Falling logically into proper

Order but upon a second reading
A glaring error will batter me about
My brain and I will feel as low as dirt
And I may be downhearted for many

Days doubting every syllable I choose
Questioning my sincerity of voice.

Riding waves and troughs
whether up or down
I'm attempting
to be
diligent.

I have a quirky dictionary with
Eccentric curious exotic words
And when lacking fresh ideas I may
Utter "jobbernowl" instead of blockhead

Or "ratbaggery" when meaning nonsense
Or "cantabank" in description of a
Mediocre balladeer — or poet —
But I would rather not have to depend

On splendiferous words to make a point
As it's better to say ordinary
Words in good order with an intention
Of expressing something worth the effort

Of reading which means I have to study
Phenomena carefully faithfully.

Queequeg the harpooner
seen through the eyes
of Ishmael in
Moby Dick is
fascinating.

There was no explanation for me to
Be so downhearted when I was so young
And had just graduated from college
Without debt after having spent my last

Year in Oxford England imbibing the
Best of the literature the English
Could offer there was no sane rationale
For the despondency I fell into

Other than my being alcoholic
Which meant that I drank to alleviate
Oppressive thinking which only served to
Give my oppressive thoughts a better grip

But I turned my life around by hitting
Bottom and by practicing principles.

A ride with the police
a detox center
a treatment center
a halfway house
a sober house
started a journey.

I can't reliably remember
The details of my thinking 40 years
Ago other than saying I was in
A treatment center for a month and a

Halfway house for five months and then I got
A room in a sober house and didn't
Have a job but was sober and meeting
With other sober drunks and I made a

A new beginning but without the numbing
Effect of alcohol I discovered
Fear fed resentment fed self-pity fed
Fear fed resentment fed self-pity fed

A barrage of oppressive emotions
And I didn't have an answer for it.

With my whole life ahead
young intelligent and free
I dug myself a
pit of misery
to hide in.

The other guys in the sober house were
Doing their best as I was but people
Who live in sober houses are starting
On perilous journeys and they are not

Entirely sane and we each took turns
Cleaning a cat litterbox but someone
Refused to do the job and I wouldn't
Because it wasn't my turn so the house

Began to fester and I didn't care
Because I was busy sleeping all day
And all night and the only reason I
Got out of bed was to have breakfast which

I did by going to a McDonald's
Restaurant that was luckily next door.

I remember
paper cups of coffee
with cream —
pancakes
with maple syrup
on Styrofoam plates.

I salvaged myself unexpectedly
By reading Herman Melville's *Moby Dick*
And in the beginning Ishmael says
When he gets a little grim about the

Mouth upon the land it's time for him to
Return to the sea and board a whaling
Vessel and on an icy blizzarding
Night Ishmael went to the Spouter Inn

With almost empty pockets and was forced
To share a bed with a tattooed savage
Queequeg a harpooner who was selling
Severed heads in New Bedford and who slept

With a tomahawk which also served him
As a tobacco pipe at his leisure.

I drank my self-obsession
away with many paper
cups of coffee with cream
by reading *Moby Dick*
at McDonald's.

Resolving to fix the litter box I
Tied a bandana about my face to
Suppress my sense of smell which was useless
And ineffective but I got busy

Becoming a waiter and a cashier
And doing other odd jobs while riding
The number 16 bus between St. Paul
And Minneapolis where I found the

Jewish Vocational Center along
University Avenue which led
To a book *Jobs in Japan* that explained
The process of getting a job teaching

English in the private language schools that
Were eagerly recruiting fresh teachers.

I boarded an airplane
and landed in Osaka
learning katakana
on the flight — not knowing
anyone in Japan.

I favor granola with blueberries
And slices of banana for breakfast
And it's a marvel of modern days that
We may find at Aldi's the cheapest of

Grocery stores blueberries coming from
Chile in January during a
Global pandemic and bananas are
OK though maybe not as exotic

And they spoil precipitously from bright
Yellow ripeness to deplorable brown
Spots on the peel and on the fruit so I
Scrounge for the bunches of green bananas

Of six or seven enough to last a
Week before they become inedible

I like a proper
amount of banana
but not too much
so I choose
small green bananas.

I believe with all my heart in nothing
And observation and evidence are
Accumulating of the cruelty
The arguing and indifference of

People between people along with willful
Ignorance including my own fickle
Eccentricities so it is hard to
Put much faith in human institutions

And I was nothing before being born
And I will become nothing after death
But somehow I am the most marvelous
Something now defying explanation

And there isn't a creation myth that
Encompasses the fact of no-thing-ness.

I am optimistic
because something
is always coming
from nothing.

Don't expect my poetry to involve
A continuing narrative from page
To page as each poem embodies its
Own cosmos and I am not attempting

To contrive a cohesive perspective
Throughout a series of pages and if
You are sensing a consistent point of
View that is because the whirlpool of a

Personality is quite similar
From day to day but my intention is
To describe a world where each happening
Is interwoven with every other

Happening without separation and
So much happens simultaneously.

The seeds of tomorrow's
growth are already
in the ground as
much is passing
away.

I appreciate the dexterity
Of my fingers because I was born with
Them and didn't do anything to earn
Their use and almost everything I do

Involves their precise sensitivity
And they create such delicacy and
So much — if not all — of my sense of touch
Is felt with the tips of my fingers and

I cannot imagine tying my shoes
Or buttoning my shirt or cutting an
Apple or feeling the texture of fleece
Or scratching my nose or typing on a

Keyboard with my toes as my toes don't do
Anything besides filling out my shoes.

I also touch
the horizon the birds
the clouds and with a
glimpse the sunrise
with my eyes.

When I am slicing a banana for
My breakfast I am happiest when not
Thinking about anything other than
Slicing a banana for my breakfast

And in fact when I am only slicing
A banana and not thinking about
Any other random obsession that
Catches me at odd moments then it is

True that I am not thinking at all but
Am only slicing a banana for
Breakfast and it is good to be doing
Something useful with my body without

The complexity of having to think
About it — which just might make me grumpy.

Do you think a
Tyrannosaur
taking a bite of
a Triceratops
was thinking about it?

Segmentation is a bane of my
Existence as I direct energy
According to the hours of a day
Consistent with the days within a month

As I need to accomplish business with
The benefit of morning clarity
Which turns the challenge of complexity
Into child's play and to manage the broad

Sweep of activity I have to watch
The dates of my publishing schedule and
Have to attend to the 15th of the
Month when I pay myself and my bills

As being a human seems to involve
The regimentation of enterprise.

The leafing of a tree
the growth of a tomato
the hunger of a
Tyrannosaur don't
involve human time.

I have seen the movies inspired by
The lure of "Jurassic Park" where the mad
And the irresponsible scientists
Brought the dinosaurs back to life using

Scraps of DNA with the intention
Of making money from tourists of the
Park and I can't get the image of the
Bald-pated Tyrannosaur out of mind

As he appears vaguely similar to
The sinewy and acrobatic bald-
Headed *karate* thugs so commonplace
In the movies but do you suppose that

A Tyrannosaur was really bald or
Might he not have had fur or feathers?

The uselessness of
a Tyrannosaur's
puny little arms
is puzzling and
funny.

My fingers and toes are so delicate
And easily harmed by inattentive
Clumsiness around the iron dumbbell
That I've positioned within my living

Room and who's to blame when I swing and smash
My toes against the unbudgeable mass
Of metal plopped on the floor under the
Edge of the coffee table or when I

Reach for the dumbbell without attending
Carefully to the speed and direction
Of my hand — and then I wince and bear a
Surge of painful toes or pinky finger

Reminding me that my appendages
Will sharply penalize my carelessness.

Did T. Rex
ever pinch
or jam a
puny arm?

I wonder whether we could attribute
The elements of personality
To a Tyrannosaur because I see
Evidence of character in Kitcat

As Kitcat will paw and disturb letters
That I keep in a bowl on my table
With the goal of seizing my attention
And Kitcat will leap onto the top of

My refrigerator and caterwaul
At me exerting I believe in his
Mind a dominance over me and I
Have read that both tyrannosaurs and cats

Possess an enhanced sense of smell so could
A Tyrannosaur have been quirky too?

How could a
Tyrannosaur be
quirky without
first thinking of
eating everyone?

Bald-pated Tyrannosaur you can't catch me
You may lumber and roar and crush a car
You may snarl with your teeth like scimitars
You stomp and blunder but can't bite me
You may shake your head but you can't get me
You may very well be the king of beasts
With every creature comprising a feast
You rule the forest but can't swallow me
With all your majesty you can't touch me
You may trot and gambol and have a ball
You stomp and smash and rip and tear and maul
But whatever you do you can't catch me
And wherever you go you won't see me
Because you are now extinct don't you see?

P.S. A Tyrannosaur may
crush cars in future movies.

Tyrannosaurs in Requiem

He gamboled upon the earth
He expressed plenty of mirth
But he's had his day
And it's fair to say
He won't have another birth.

I would not be the person who I am
Without reading the sonnets of Shakespeare
Even though I've come to see the crazy
Houdini-encumbering rhyming scheme

At the ends of his lines to be a waste
Of effort and a frustration of free
Expression but nevertheless the pith
And passion of his lovely delicate

Little poems indelibly affected
Me — and I wouldn't be who I am if
I hadn't read Japanese poetry

As they astonished me by putting so
Much sensitivity in so few words.

Shakespeare and
the Japanese
fashion poetry
like keenly
sharp daggers.

I also would not be exploring the
World as I do today if I hadn't
Absorbed *Siddhartha* by the novelist
Hermann Hesse as the suffering and the

Questing to end suffering with the use
Of meditation reverberated
As I was perusing pages in a
High school library — and I might have been

Swallowed up in a mire of self-pity
If I hadn't had the exquisite shock
Of reading Herman Melville's *Moby Dick*
That made me forget myself entirely

By enticing me with the exotic
Narrative of Ishmael the sailor.

Two Hermans
moved me
by writing
vibrantly.

To get a laugh from my friends in every
Month of last year I have touted my post-
Traumatic February Disorder
And today is February 1st and

Not a phantom put-on February
But a real February so I pulled
On the long underwear to go under
My jeans and slipped on two pairs of socks and

Two hats and elephantine mittens and
Drove to the park for my outdoor meeting
And saw a touch of ice on the concrete
From yesterday's drizzle but it was just

A little below freezing as I was
Wrapped like an eggroll and feeling silly.

Reality is
usually
different
from what
I think.

We gathered around the cheery fire in
Our container at Pioneer Park and
Began our meeting of sober drunks with
The view of Stillwater below us and

Of the winding river valley into
The distance and coincident with our
Conversation one of us heard the spring
Songs of an American Crow of a

Black-capped chickadee of a white-breasted
Nuthatch and of a Northern Cardinal
But I only recognized the crow as
My ears are not very sensitive and

As we were each speaking — one at a
Time — I did hear the Northern Cardinal.

Without Fran
alerting us to the
cardinal I would
never have
heard it.

At our Monday morning meeting we talk
About yesterday and tomorrow and
Today with the point being that to live
Well in today we need freedom from the

Burdens of yesterday and tomorrow
From remorse and anxiety which are
Phantoms of the mind as for some reason
It is easy to be negative and

Hard to be optimistic just as it's
Easy to hear a crow but tricky to
Pick up the cardinal as I needed
Direction to hear the cardinal and

So I need to practice principles and
Rely on a power greater than me.

We have already
made it through most
of our first year of
hobo meetings
in the park.

At the beginning of February
Under an overcast sky within a
Culture that is intoxicated with
Technology and media and the

News cycle it's easy to forget that
The earth the sun and the moon are doing
Their interweaving dance beyond the clouds
And tomorrow in the north we will reach

The midmost point between the winter and
Spring equinoxes which the Celtic tribes
Celebrated with a festival as
"Imbolc" or "Brigid's day" for the marking

Of the beginning of spring even as
The ground is quiescent under the snow.

The weaving
of fire air
water earth
continues
quietly.

Perhaps the roots of the trees are waking
And seeds in the ground are poised for growing
And the bears in their dens are stirring as
Daylight is arising earlier and

Lasting longer into the evening but
The cold is persistent and heavy on
The land impelling yet a sheltering
Indoors and a separation from the

Zest of activity sweating under
A blazing sun and thusly this is a
Time for asking what is essential and
What is no longer worthy of doing

And how are circumstances transforming
And how do I need to adapt myself?

The opacity
of an overcast
sky is weighty
with questions.

Am I working hard to accomplish goals?
Has enough of my stridency been tamed?
Do I still need to prove my worth to me?
And I have only to ask the questions

To understand the effort involved in
Making something of myself by getting
Ahead of the competition using
The vigor of focused intelligence

To be proud and comfortable later
And I really don't know how to behave
Differently as society does
Impose its pressures but a part of me

Is exhausted and dissatisfied and
Blundering about for liberation.

Random thought
mesmerizing
emotion
keeps
happening.

It's 2 a.m. and the cat wants to play
As he is gamboling upon my bed
Pouncing and biting until I say "hey
It's way too early and you have been fed"
As I'm feeling the pulsation of blood
Throbbing at my temples on the pillow
And Kitcat jumps to the floor with a thud
And what he thinks he's doing yes I know
Because I've gotten him used to playing
When I will rise from bed before the dawn
When I brush and rub him while I'm singing
When he loves his brushing and has his fun
When he gets excited and wants to fight
When I slap his paws and he tries to bite.

Kitcat had reason
to think I was getting up
from sleeping because
I rose from bed twice
to write notes for a poem.

I dread the twilight zone in the middle
Of the night when I wake from sleeping and
My mind has the opportunity to
Run away with me and this morning I

Was drowsy on the edge of slumber yet
Nervous energy from yesterday was
Enough to spur a subconscious hunt for
Exorbitant words for a trivial

Poem and in my ambivalence thoughts
Acquired metal-studded cleats that poked
Into my consciousness and compelled my
Rising from bed to scrawl syllables on

Notepaper because I can't rely on
Nighttime memory to survive the night.

A tinge of agony
over whether I should
rise and make a note
or forget the thought
tends to wake me up.

When I pinch the tires of my bicycle
Laid against the chairs in my dining room
I detect squishiness instead of the
Roadworthy firmness that I desire and

Seeing the bicycle laid staidly in
My dining room everyday has had a
Subconscious and subversive influence
On my temperament as winter drags on

As the stationary bike within my
Living room has provided a sturdy
Service as I have listened to music
On headphones and pumped my legs for an hour

Every day but I want to face the wind
Again and climb the hill into Houlton.

I am looking forward
to hearing peeper frogs
and seeing tulips
from my bike
in the spring.

The branches of the
maple are swaying in
the wind under a
shining blue sky but
snow comes tomorrow.

—*Tekkan*

www.ingramcontent.com/pod-product-compliance
Lightning Source LLC
Chambersburg PA
CBHW040421100526
44589CB00021B/2782